SELF-PORTRAIT AS OTHELLO

Jason Allen-Paisant is a Jamaican poet and academic who works as a senior lecturer in Critical Theory and Creative Writing at the University of Manchester. He's the author of two poetry collections, *Thinking with Trees* (Carcanet), winner of the 2022 OCM Bocas Prize for poetry, and *Self-Portrait as Othello* (Carcanet), winner of the 2023 Forward Prize for Best Collection. His memoir, *The Possibility of Tenderness*, will be published by Hutchinson Heinemann in 2024 and a monograph, *Engagements with Aimé Césaire*, will also appear in 2024, with Oxford University Press. He lives in Leeds with his wife and two children.

ALSO
BY
JASON ALLEN-PAISANT
FROM
CARCANET

Thinking with Trees
(2021)

Self-Portrait As Othello

Jason Allen-Paisant

CARCANET POETRY

First published in Great Britain in 2023 by
Carcanet
Alliance House, 30 Cross Street
Manchester, M2 7AQ
www.carcanet.co.uk

A CIP catalogue record for this book is
available from the British Library.

ISBN 978 1 80017 310 1

Book design by Andrew Latimer
Printed in Great Britain by SRP Ltd, Exeter, Devon

The publisher acknowledges financial
assistance from Arts Council England.

CONTENTS

To those who live in choreography, in multiplicity, to those always inhabiting the liminal space.

For Keturah, as ever.

SELF-PORTRAIT AS OTHELLO

I am an alien from outer space
and I ain't got no home,
I'm living in my briefcase.
I am a hitchhiker,
hitching and hiking
straight from Africa.
— Lee 'Scratch' Perry

Qu'est-ce la patrie ? Ne serait-elle pas justement cet endroit qui est à la
fois […] le vrai et à la fois le fictionné ; à la fois ce qui a lieu et qui n'a
plus lieu […]?
— Caroline Guiela Nguyen

I need to reach [my father] the only way I know – by memory and
invention – see him at his best […] in order to lay his ghost to rest.
— Fred D'Aguiar

RINGING OTHELLO

How could I resurrect you to speak,
when your burial is in no ground
that I can pilgrimage to, except that
I have been to Venice and known
you walking in that place, as if something
had been left undone. Presumptuous to think
that I could make you speak.
Who am I?

But I feel sometimes
that our destinies conjoin, that your life,
unfinished, is lived also through mine.
Your silence is a haunting, brothers are wanting,
people are waiting to hear. I conjure you
furiously.

I

I am five. I sit on the barbecue*
dangling my feet chewing grass straw

like Brother B*, boy following
man; my heart races every time a car

blows horn or pulls up, thinking
that must be my father a him that

come look fi me yes him come.
The people fly past and Mama* runs

to look and she stares and peers and
the people will not stop flying past

like the whirlwind like the hurricane
but daddy was not in the wind.

We sit on the barbecue
Brother B and I

twirling grass straws in our mouths
watching the sun go down.

You pour out water from
the drum into bath pan and tin;

the mento band
plucks out a tune

in the church below the hill.
It's night time;

tonight I will get into
the spirit, rise from my body

and fly away
like Mother Pusey.

When she claps those hands
each clap sends silence

through the galaxy
lifts her through clouds singing

how I got over falling and
rising all these years.

I sit on the barbecue
Brother B and I listening

to your drum pan and water;
the church below

the hill catches
the spirit,

the body a thing
of weight falling

through sky.

Tweed-jacketed
on the terrace of a cocktail bar
a Jamaican country boy
    fly as a motha
    But look at him though... I just
    can't...
The Prada lenses fake
    straight plastic same as the day
they came out the factory
Him feel expensive him look
    fit for de part

At Hi-Lo
the Jamaican Eating House
Crazy Andy takes him in
to sip rum and listen
to rocksteady

In a version of this story
he manages to come back home
to see you before you die
Mama—at Christmas he's not alone—
but that version isn't to happen

Instead he's reading Baudelaire's
Les Fleurs du mal
through the English winter

Among the dreaming spires
you're the truth he runs from

I'm going to Paris Mama
    and I cannot sleep tonight
watching the stars   night comes
    untying the cords of my tongue

rabashundai! the secret place
    the void the bush *shalla-mashundai!*
I give myself over to a shout
    blooming in pain

rabashundai! the secret place
    the bush of Babel
I started speaking French at thirteen
    and pronounced every sound perfectly

the vowels rolled off my tongue
    and I was untied and I
soared away from my body
    and in the bush my mother she couldn't find me

in the bush I had a part fit for me
    in the bush shooting bird and going river
something seized me
    and every day was a day of Pentecost

my vowels how they wrapped
    their arms around me

I'm going to Paris at last
    Mama's grandson
and I cannot sleep tonight
    watching the stars

Pas de Calais plumes against my skin
    will I learn to speak here
a tongue of loss and forsaking
    my mother and father left me

and Mama took me in
    the varnish of the fields
a lynx at my heels
    nowhere and then

fourmillante cité beside me
    Paris *tout d'un coup*
I take up my room at the École normale
    I speak the language but the space

don't know my body
    a room on the third floor of
the *internat* 10 sq. metres a landscape
    of speaking voices nobody

in sight presence of mould in
    the ceiling words *incandescent*
fines sablures d'un rêve Fleurs du
    mal flowers blooming in the dark

a damp room on the third floor
    École normale supérieure
no sound in that hallway but in my blood
    how sharply loneliness cuts the body

my woman walks so dirgefully beside me
    I will always be a stranger here the thing is the bloody
thing is I didn't realize it didn't
    realize that Black was a different language

that poor Porus was a different
    language that no picket fence no paper
and papa was a different
    language that going to the theatre

every other night going broke
    was my new language to act bourgeois
and find my bourgeois style
    the plush-carpeted Comédie Française

Salle Pleyel for music opera and theatre
    no heads like mine to watch Phèdre die only
one Black man in the room who rises from
    the orchestra to salute me fist bump in air

one other black man in the room speaks
    my language the language of performer
to crowd and wooow did they like it the looks
    aaah trying to find whiteness in my blackness

come on bredren my Jamaican brother says to me
    black people don't go opera you know this

I call you daddy *bois d'ébène*
pieces of scattered wood

you break me into a million parts
and everything I am is you

I wander in search of you a trunk of tree
reaching my eye faint in the fat of fog

mon passé est là qui me montre et me dérobe son visage
blurred and calm it stands there

between retreat and outline face keen to speak
mon avenir est là qui me tend la main

I try to touch you the space between
outer space and inner music

disappeared and blasted pieces to the east
and west to the north and south

I go in search of you to touch to speak
light and music sounds of stars of space

daddy daddy inna mi soulcase

I see the woman's lips the eagerness
   in her eyes a surprising *métisse*
intello et jolie a proud nose
   a smile of leeches in a perfect circle

a flash of assent in her eyes
   I walked into the stinging of desire
arranged words into an arsenal *if you wanna roll*
   wid a pro then roll with me baby

but she was already mine
   my guide on the journey through the Inferno
in the Latin Quarter we kissed passionately
   then met again at a café in the Marais

an evening filled with awkwardness
   with nervous questions I made the night
unsubtle driving the charm away
   would I score did she want to by miracle

I'm back in her bed I pray her copper skin
   is really there cat-purring against mine
but shame the fly got stuck in my brain
   like every time the mask no use for

the shame fly droning jabbing at my temples
   go back to Porus where you from
and tell yourself pretender this ain't your category
   she sees a Frenchman when she looks at me

my Jamaicanness wiped out like my accent
   a lie to go with my tweed
but I couldn't dislodge the shame fly from my brain
   all she saw was someone who fucked up the mood

smile of leeches perfect circle of pain
    a woman's lips the eagerness in her eyes
we descend stairs of stone
    the woman I had kissed in the middle of the street

is here underground in the club
    glory and praise the woman I had kissed in the north is
here in the south and yes
    I am going back to seek her a shard in my palm

douleur the oozing oooo-ing of the ouuuu
    and the aaa of the grinding
the sound of pain is a winding whining
    dou dou douleur doudou dance wid me
is a wine in my mouth is the sexiness of the words

is a land of sin of pain the neon lights
    the thirst of skin on skin smell of hunger
violon dingue sounds in the night-sea
    going down underneath stones

coming back up ain't sure but down
    down down in the locked deep
these stones be watching me my jumper's too ugly
    my locks don't fit the shame fly won't quit

my head don't stand right not suave
    smooth small my sebaceous glands ooze monsters
my head don't fit I don't fit right inside it
    and what about my arms? I can't control

the way they bend cannot find home for my body
    inside my body inside Porus inside Paris
inside the skin of my small house of Mommy
    of missiles of mop sticks flying

I've drowned my pain *tonight like yesterday*
    like so many other nights from bar to bar from
hole to hole from drink to drink
    I've drowned my pain crying

daddy daddy when daddy

I pull myself through tight spaces through the twists
    and turns of the Marais' dim alleyways
the locks won't do but I insist
    I sleep the days away

no-one can see me ghost actor
    will it be worth it will it be worth
it my woman has left me no ground left under
    me my granny now lies in the earth

September spiralled into October October
    into a circle of shadows show me the hidden side
of the script the question of the futile terror-
    ises me there are many sighs

bodies mainly mine I see now rushing
    around on the edge of Acheron
hurrying to one place then fleeing
    in opposite direction

show me the hidden side of the script I want
    the kind of life that can be read
not piddling paltry mooching along instead
    why do I always have to be translated

never well represented
    I need to find a place to be spectacular
in this place I am too many things and
    life is easier when you singular

at nights in the *K-Fèt**
    École normale supérieure
hair dancing over faces like flames
    come to me the whole o' unnu

come let me fill you with my desire
    I am hungry for talk I am a stranger
we smile fake scream fake dance fake
    the bodies eager the bodies white

marble statues inna me story book
    white body of my learning yes come now
you and I be my Desdemona on stage
    in the *K-Fèt* let us dance all night under the light
your hair of snakes will worm and knot us together

no light no air the music is my body on yours

September spiralled into October October
   into a circle of shadows
Look down on this child
   even inna my dream mi a beg

daddy daddy when daddy
   absence and loss meet inna di miggle
miggle finger to you

me voici dans la foule accepting big invitations
    Odéon Salle Pleyel the plush carpeted
Comédie-Française a place in the upper stalls
    Le Speakeasy on Champs-Elysées

40 euro for an entrée *aspirationiste, assume !*
    you must feel it inna di Speakeasy
duo of foie gras and half-cooked tuna
    live jazz drinking up Veuve Clicquot

saxophone and piano riffin miles into space
    you must feel it this acting
then when they carry the bill she pays cash
    2000 odd BLOUSE AND SKIRT!
cash money flashing pon di table

her daughter criss like money my body weak
    you must feel like you could!
bout daddy is a civil engineer *mon cul*
    you've got to be what you LOATHE

what you scorn a box-bout harbourless
    says Brathwaite nice word *harbourless spade*
bastard pickney embrace each-o-we-a-different-
    faada story embrace NO-DAD
absence and loss inna de miggle

throw way de dyam tweed
    put ON YOUR GOLD CHAIN
and rock that pendant with the studs the hefty cross
    step out inna you dung-cyah swag them girls rush
you inna the club and outside

the Violon Dingue from 12 to 5 inna de morning

In Prague   a hot summer's day on the Charles Bridge the river's
demented blades of sunlight   a yellowness compelling me to jump
I split the air like a horse's stride the moist   legs of the morning
emerge like islands on the surface of the sea   my desire beats

like a thoroughbred   we hunted carnal pleasure my friend and I
I agreed it was a game of healing and transgression   my self was
lurking   ready to step out of the shade   I was the ultimate in Black
my body swelled up   till kaya hair thick lips and African nose

filled the universe as the waters came into me   my self emerged
from Prague's river   Then the night swayed its hips
into the heaven of a dancehall   like towers my desires rose   *get up*
I heard them speak   rising into the darkness as the enigma of a woman

passed my way   her thighs mantled in coital light   she danced
I could feel within my chest her surprised command   It was obeah
possessing her soul   The rest of the night   I was the ancient king
laughing over the city   I was gable and arch

A horse was neighing
threatening to break the barrier of my skin

to allow a shout to get out and in
breaking the wall of my skin crying out and in

I call you daddy *bois d'ébène* pieces of scattered wood
disappeared and blasted scattered

to the east and west to the north and south
mon passé est là qui me montre et me dérobe son visage

Un-Dad Un-Dad I ain't died I split divide
& recreate I ain't one I multiplied

On the Ponte di Rialto I watch myself glide on distances of times
and seas   Rialto shivers like the lagoon's contours   like the dream
of marble in my veins   waves gliding to the distant country
and back to this bridge   to the country where I first learnt the name Rialto

through Shakespeare taught in a Jamaican tongue   where I let it ring
echo and disappear into time   now I come and find it real
La Serenissima   my senses soar   like the flame in Bellini's reds
like the curling flames of Tiziano and Giorgione Tiepolo and Tintoretto

the light over the Canal Grande   *Il paese che un dì sognai...*
già lungo tempo lo cercai... between houses whose walls never tire
of the water's tongue   *rapimento* of skirts   the air filled with mosaics
tesserae of dreams   how they move!   thronging this city
around whose corners the mind turns endlessly   never tiring
each lapping of the lagoon's tongue a page   *tessera dei miei sogni*

I sit on the barbecue when the bath water pour and the
sun get cold and the orange water soak the ground

the drum water make music and evening crack and ooze
like mango. I kick the air, a grass straw in my mouth.

The night meeting building, hands clapping, feet tapping.
Tonight I'm rising from my body and before you know it

I'm flying through the clouds. Ever see a man
travel more seen more lands than this boy from Coffee Grove,

where hope is like the dry root of a red dirt rockstone?
Now a doing road, dancing through Prague Paris Rome.

Auch in München bin ich zu Hause. Can you believe me
bouncing up into Oxford? Every weekend I paint that town

red, and I don't mind all the whiteness and I don't mind all
the tweed, and I don't make all the posh talking bother me.

Watch me speaking four languages outside the club. Watch me
in Prague among the patina-streaked marble. I am dancing

through Europe actor and spectator in a carnival of bodies.
A doing road in Venice, where the black Moor head is placed

on doors and wrung by hand every day. Florence Bordeaux
and Nice. A doing road. My future, the shadow peeping

through fog, the shadow speaking, seeking me.
Un-Dad with you I feel death and I feel birth, I have never

felt them so close together. With you I am born
and stand looking down at myself as if coming into the world

for the first time. Me is rising standing up straight,
ready to run, to bound. What I am now stands on its feet.

II

THE PICTURE AND THE FRAME

I.

I have found no word for the effect of the light on the water other than *mare=ballerina*, the one Gino Severini invented.

*

Nothing makes sense until it makes sense in the body, till the body is present at the making-sense.

*

There's a set of people selling small things on the Piazza San Marco. What should we call these small things, since what they actually are doesn't matter? They throw these things in the air. I approach one, asking what they are. *Lanza*, he says. A toy for kids. For demonstration, he throws one, catching it back. *8 euros*, he says. There's this set of people. I've seen them seeing with their feet, their backs, their entire bodies. I've seen them knowing when to run from the police before the police are in sight. Have you seen them too?

*

Eight years I've been trying to name this recognition expressed in my flesh.

*

Mare=Ballerina is supposedly about a dancer, one who, in her movement, evokes the crashing of the waves on the seashore. For me, it evoked the light over the Canal and its houses, the Venice I saw, wondering what The Moor saw, that Moor who arrived here at such a point in the 16th century that he could have been at home in Carpaccio's *Miracle of the Relic of the Cross at the Rialto Bridge*. That he could have been *that* gondolier, the sharp looking dude. That Venice, that canal, that light seen from the oriental windows.

*

The Venice expressed in my flesh, as if the spirit of the sea of back home was also here.

*

Where you from? The people selling the small things greet me like this when my eyes meet theirs. It's the only way to greet, as if to say, *why, who, you, here – you who see me.*

Ali, 21, from Senegal guesses at where I'm from in Africa. He sells bracelets.

Buy a bracelet to support me, pour me soutenir. We bond through the French language. We move around in the wide world, forced into fluidity. It's not my style but, of course. He gives me an additional one for free. *Porte-bonheur. Pour les enfants.*

2.

In Veronese's *Feast at the Home of Levi*, conceived in fact as a depiction of *The Last Supper* before the artist's brush with the Inquisition, a young, dark-skinned man dressed in red tunic and turban shares the frame with Jesus and the apostles.

All of a sudden, with Veronese's hedonistic canvas, one enters a time without really entering it. The painting becomes a joke on the viewer. A door to a chamber is shown without any key whatsoever to access it. One's only consolation is to say, *I have seen that we were here, so normally here, in another time.*

Without any witness (writing, inscriptions, books, legends) tying that time to the present, all the stories have to be invented—reinvented.

*

In the window of Nardi, the jeweller's, there are Blackamoor brooches. There are rings made of diamonds and rubies with miniature heads of turbaned Moors in sculpted ebony.

*

The intervening history of the representation of my body in text.

*

For Veronese, this painting was all about invention, and for it, he took huge license with theological doctrine.

*

There are Moor heads everywhere. We're not talking about this.

*

One wonders what kind of a character he is, this red-turbaned African man present at the banquet of a Renaissance prince. He's talking to a fat white man dressed in fancier robes. The fat dude looks into the distance distractedly. One can't help but notice the wily look on African dude's face, but only after a while do you notice his hand reaching into the other man's bag. Disappointing to say the least. The other African figures in the canvas occupy subservient roles, like pages, but they're also comfortably there. They're looking people in the eye, even having conversation. Ambiguous. But with ambiguity, I find myself stepping into a different history of representation. Ambiguity is a fucking revolution. It's almost overwhelming.

*

All I have is invention. All I could ever do is invent. I was tired of invention.

*

There's all the stuff that the European viewer can't see, all the stuff they haven't allowed themselves to see.

*

The Moor remains invisible, despite the obsession with his body.

SELF-PORTRAIT AS OTHELLO I

I.

Undeterred by father's anger
& disapproval
she thinks that we

should have every right
to be in love –
Venice aristocrat,

African soldier.
Her belief,
this version of myself,

a future
for her and for me   why should I
always fight?

Raised by tales of Barbary
and Guinea, she offered her country
in exchange for my stories –

encounters with death,
my childhood as soldier
on the River Gambia.

2.

The jealous white boy's venom
was language
even now very now

an old black ram is
tupping your white ewe
When I spoke, my sound

was white gaze.
The very real thing
is that you should not be

too large in this space.
Iago the language
controlling the play.

And what he was saying, thousands
were saying and thinking.
Here I am now; we see

how it ends; yes, we're freed
from the play,
and still – dare I believe

that I was no fetish, that this
my body was real to you?
As faith crumbled

I thought you loved my storytelling
more than me,
Mandinka warrior *della Guinea*;

and the demon became *my own face.*

What Shakespeare did not write about. The story he was unable to tell.

*

Othello is a real structure of feeling taking shape, which the world had never known. How could it have? The world was not yet world.

*

When he wrote *Othello*, the slave trade had been happening for seven decades, with the Pope's blessing.

*

I'm haunted as much by the character Othello as by the silences in the story.

*

Othello the Moor. It was the tax raised from the church in the name of Ferdinand's and Isabella's 'just and holy war' against the Kingdom of Granada, and Islam, that financed Columbus' first voyage to the Americas.

*

Five centuries later, why does *Othello* offer up so easy a template for this precarity, for this endless negotiation? *Texte, mon corps.*

*

Why does it offer up so easy a template for the shame produced in my body?

OTHELLO WALKS

Othello walks through
the marbled city;
his skin betrays him.

He is striving against
badmind. This is Othello's life –
trying to beat the odds.
And what is asked of him?

To be *more fair than black*
If virtue no delighted
beauty lack.

              *

You're real to me as I
ring your name; more present
than the living. I imagine

scenarios that may have brought
you to this city. In one of them,
you're following your father's

footsteps across the oceans.
You're looking for him in the wind.

SELF-PORTRAIT AS OTHELLO II

The Black body is signed as physically and psychically open space... A space not simply owned by those who embody it but constructed and occupied by other embodiments. Inhabiting it is a domestic, hemispheric... transatlantic... international pastime. There is a playing around in it.
Dionne Brand, *A Map to the Door of No Return.*

You left home for a wandering lust for pain
    had driven you to the edge of yourself & wanting
to open the windows of life you decided to migrate to this
    country. You came for a different sound

the quaintness of gestures of faces & food. New tongues
    are something like trophies *faccia* faces *façades...*
The façade hides things you like this each new word
    an erotic death your language grows with buried things.

What does it mean to be *far more fair than black?*
    Education speech dress learning. You have the brawn
of an intellectual rude boy sturdier in brain-work
    than in war. Know streets and livity talk Shakespeare

Baudelaire Dante and Nietzsche talk sound system. What actually
    is the language of where you're from? It's that familiarity
with rough life that eye of struggle that smell of fight
    hardness of speech a coming up vibe Oxford and all

that she likes so invites you to visit at Christmas three whole days
    with family and one party to the next but they think
it's going to pass this fascination with the dark-skinned boy surely
    she'll come around find someone of her kind   *when she is sated.*

Alvise Da Cada Mosto, a Venetian, in the service of Don Henry of Portugal, informs us in his preface, that he was the first navigator from the noble city of Venice who had sailed on the ocean beyond the Straits of Gibraltar, to the southern parts of Negroland, and Lower Ethiopia. These voyages are the oldest extant and were first printed at Venice in 1507.

He considered the rivers Senegal and Rio Grande to be branches of the Niger, by which means the Europeans might open a trade with the rich kingdoms of Tombuto and Melli on that river, and thus bring gold from the countries of the Negroes, by an easier, safer, and more expeditious manner, than as conveyed by the Moors of Barbary by land, over the vast and dangerous deserts that intervene between the country on the Niger and Senegal rivers, and Barbary. As, by the account of Leo, salt is the most valuable commodity throughout the countries of the Negroes, Ramusio proposed that the ships should take in cargoes of salt at the island of Sal and thence supply the countries on the Niger, which was reported to be navigable for 500 miles into the interior; and that they should bring back gold and slaves in return; the latter to be brought to market at St Jago, another of the Cape de Verd islands, where they would be immediately bought up for the West Indies.

WHO IS OTHELLO? I

Raised on the River Gambia,
I learned to row in the Venetian way
dive with amphibian lungs &
fight with hands and sword.

Men came looking for us,
promising residences
on the Canal Grande,
estates on the mainland,

jobs as *condottieri*.
At 28, I was in Venice;
at 30, a commander of land armies.
Otello, from Old high German *Otto*

meaning 'rich and prosperous',
I am here and I'm striving.
Otello della Guinea
is my name.

I stopped in at many ports where
sailors cavorted.
I stopped in at Venice
and it became my home.

WHO IS OTHELLO? II

The decree of 1489 distinguished
between white and black slaves
for the first time

And in the midst of that you
as a noble Black in Venice
saraceno nobile

contracted because of
your skills in war
a sailor and sea captain

Tall and sculptural
your body
split the wind boldly

Condottiero
you excel in battles
but not in the city

SELF-PORTRAIT AS OTHELLO III

I was called *bois d'ébène*
I am dismembered
I look for the different parts of myself

in the world's oceans
in the black blood of Europe's
monuments, in their sweat stains

In the nervous system
of the bridge – Rialto –
I sound my cells

I have been here before and heard
the lips of the water against the houses
seen the light of the Canal

This place is no stranger
The vowels planed from the ocean
dissolve on my tongue

A patina-streaked conqueror
wants to be my father
I birth you with my seed

My name is in crisis
I am scattered all over
your cities, Europe!

SELF-PORTRAIT AS OTHELLO IV

In death I relinquish my masculinity –
same one that killed Desdemona.
What need did I have for honour,
when it meant nothing?
I embrace the incongruence
of my intersectional self.
Much better. Oh, and one other thing –

I've been leaning in-
to my mother tongue.

SELF-PORTRAIT AS OTHELLO V

I am neither a *thugz* nor a *shotta*
All I wanted was not
to be invisible, to have face

Here, I am anything I want –
I make myself
They want *stories*

Stories are everything
for my audience
I tell stories
That she likes
can't get enough

She wanted in I mean
she wanted in-
to an outside world

Iago's voice
was too loud
too controlling

Public school boys sit
in parliamentary green chairs
in the MCR*

their accent so round
so sonorous, so full
of the knowledge that money bought
they know *every* place
have done *every*thing

And me
my knowledge was
undefinable desire
for a country – *a* country,
the breathing of the ocean;
hunger not for *hair-breadth 'scapes*
but for *stories*
the liquid of language

the oversized penis juts out

into a pool

of guffaws

I laugh embarrassed

at myself   there you are   you TOO

are laughing

am I visible—   this my body

on an operating table?

disown the terror   of your laugh   I am

a mound

of stone—   they tell me   they were just

being silly   just this oversized

penis on a life-size black doll   they tell me   they didn't

realise   for isn't she lovely   how they danced pranced

gyrated

how they   ran in the streets

around the fountain   in the Parisian night   at Place Gambetta

how I saw the pictures   though no one said a word

& how I pretended that what I saw

was not seen

PLACE DE LA NATION

For Ahmaud Arbery

You leave the house and head to the gym. You ride the metro.
You listen to some music. You read a novel
           try to act cool
like you belong here   you're so French

You travel in the underground   going from side to side of the city
The darkness helps   the white noise in a crowd
           The crowd must be thick
or you will see your body

           raising suspicions by walking
                    you do not want that

But then you get to another part of the city
           and re-emerge, and you're hit with images again
of yourself in the space, and yourself

           is two beautiful dark-skinned children
just innocently sitting on a bench waiting,
not bothering anyone, just waiting &
           you want to weep because they are so beautiful

           and nobody should be wrong to be
so beautiful in this world
& that beauty lies there knowing that one day   it will lift
itself from their bodies
           like a question
You mourn the future loss of this being,
so full in space, so occupying, so sitting before you
on the bench. You re-emerge into this life
raising suspicions again.

*

They're from Mauritania they say, brother and sister,
   They sit there on a park bench
along the busy way &
look at me   with doe eyes   a look of discovery

in the fine grain of skin, the perfect lines of teeth
the stillness, as if no language had yet been made
        as if the first day on earth.
        They look into this world
deciding whether to enter

nobody should be wrong to be
        so beautiful in this world

And he's running right now…
There he goes right now!

        *

So you try   not to act too muscular   not to look too big
        muscular looks very threatening on your skin

you want to walk hard, jog hard, be hard
but today you think about your mother

you owe it to her to protect her from this
   what you can do   what can be done to you

you've just come out of the gym   you feel fit
you feel strong   you feel large and full of blood

but you small up yourself   and keep going
            you read endless messages about your body
you're consuming your body
All the images fill you

And he's running right now…
There he goes right now!

PUNTED DOWN THE CHERWELL

If my mother had told me a white man
would serve you I would have said

you lie serve you over there
that you would be over the white man
in his own country

Oh colonial in defeat
image of centuries swallowed
look

Look at them teeth how they white
as I sail down the river Cherwell
with a white man punting my punt

III

THE LAST TIME

Sunday and we're at church
You're wearing that cotton dress
I've seen in my earliest memory
the fuchsia one with
the bulbous flowers

There's dried food on it
& I doubt you're aware
& I say nothing

You're wearing your yard slippers
Likewise I say nothing
Think of the breaking of the shell
we call self

Over the year to come
fresh lines will reshape
the landscape of your eyes
Mommy will watch them form
I'll be away in Oxford
making life

Right now your mind
settles in the church –
still familiar
Thirty years ago you and I
were already here
This is what I know –
like flowing water
no beginning or end

THE NIGHT OF THE DEATH

Check me out simmerin
  cross the dance floor
5000 miles
   away
     to house music

Mommy   you really could have
picked up the phone

My smile won't go
I slow down and
   the world
      returns only
slowly
Mama dead just so

Can I speak to someone
   other than these
Erasmus girls shimmying
on the dance floor?

Mommy you really could have
   picked up the phone

I'm dancing
through the Facebook message
to house music

They're asking me
Are you alright?
   in Paris
   dancing

Tommy   Mama dead
The Facebook message
   in the *K-Fêt*   École normale supérieure

I didn't return home
to you waiting for me
   two months
   Mama
   travelling

and I
couldn't afford the plane ticket
but

here   I am
dancing
I'm in a café in Paris
   École normale supérieure
   these girls shimmying beside me

Mommy
you could have
picked up the phone
   not a Facebook message
I would have paid

HOMECOMING

I have finally worked up
the fare and here I am.

The red doors greet me,
the small veranda,

the ledges with steel exposed,
a house's gangrene.

The old curtains still there
holding in the darkness.

The new room, the extension started
and suspended.

The moulding under the window
roughcast and showy –

a heart invoking Love.
and the coconut tree still

standing in the backyard drawing life
from my navel string

planted there by you
digging *Lord   help me care him*

for I don't young no more.
Are those your hands

still digging?
I feel them slipping

you slipping
into the red belly

of the ground
Mama

the dividing air
closing

behind you.

TO FIND MAMA'S VOICE

I look for Mama's voice in Dropbox
and old devices, anywhere
I may have inadvertently
captured the sound
back when I didn't think
her voice would be everywhere
and yet nowhere to be found.

The real thing?
I hear it all the time –
right here, filling the space.
What if I could produce the grain,
the texture and timbre by some fluke,
one day, by some intervention, some freak
of nature, and something was on hand to record?

One day I may open my mouth to speak
and her voice will leap out, so
strangers who never knew her
might hear it. I must find it. But where?
Mommy has no recordings.
Cousin Lee has not preserved it either.
No one thought we would want it.

And why have on tape
what we have in our heads
all the time? What would be the use
of sharing this sound?
To run Mama's voice over the tips
of our fingers, to know her now
as we've never known her before?

ON THE BUS TO GAMBETTA

Black woman sitting
on rear bench of no. 26
between Place d'Italie and Gambetta,
dressed in *boubou* and *gele*;
at Cours de Vincennes she sits
alone behind; at Maraîchers,
she snores, lying down,
her hand gripping the pole.
See the lurch of the edge.
A woman pretends to read,
Parisienne with stiff book;
I watch her lips curve
into almost-laugh, her eyes
sideways glitter, while the woman
balances at the edge,
hand working in her sleep.
Terminus. Tous les passagers
sont invités à descendre.
She sits up – a quick hand
straightens headscarf – joins the flow
of passengers melting into the
moving sounds of the city,
her floaty *bazin* disappearing into
the plane-lined street.

DOOR OF NO RETURN

a name ... marked out territory... the Door of No Return, a place of
emptied beginnings –
Dionne Brand

I.

There is a first namelessness,
        an absence of territory, of
                land of water of rock;
the second is the haunting of the first.

    I bear   his name, meaning
        stories without a body;
                he disappeared before I was born.

Disappearing is part of our way in the world;
    we understand this world through disappearance.

2.

I knew the absence
of our fathers had to do

with the affliction of
leaving

with that
Door of No Return

3.

I took the name *Paisant,*
meaning some old
old French for *peasant.*
It's the name of my Breton
wife. Years before I met her,

I had imagined Breton ancestors
who'd fled Guadeloupe
during the Revolution – 1789 –
and ended up in Jamaica.
Tu as des aïeux français, sans doute,

a French colleague had once whispered
to me at the Alliance Française in Kingston;
she couldn't wrap her mind around
how I sounded, as if I'd been born
with this language – it was her solution;

it opened up a room in me
that has never closed. In this space
I would resolve the issue of my name
and of my absent father –
so, at least, I thought.

4.

In Paris, I met a man by the name of Richard Allen at a dinner hosted by an American sista, who probably thought that our surname was a special reason for connecting us. Richard Allen – from Georgia Alabama; went to Morehouse. Where he grew up, they had a lot of lynchings back in the day, he tells me. We speak about two different climates, two different suns; about the sameness of our different histories; and wonder if through us the dead retrace their steps around the globe. How funny the arbitrariness of our arbitrary name. We wonder how related we are, if at all. Our ancestors were young boys and girls 'owned' by Englishmen who crossed the oceans to trade in African flesh. His great-great-great grandfather was sold to one of these men, after arriving at the port of Charleston. And here we are now, across the seas, in Paris, both of us dreaming big, searching for something great, a sense of ourselves we didn't find back home. We were looking for space and seemed to find something of it here. He's living in *another* white man's country. He's followed so many other men and women who've come here in a first great post-slavery journey, back out, looking for the womb of the world, our land, our territory, our father's waters.

5.

My father, I address you, as you crouch
in the dark corner. When they made you turn
seven times around the Tree of Forgetting, none
of them could have imagined
the outer limits of this forgetting,
how it spread into time.

The Hebrews, we're told, wept together
when they remembered Jerusalem, but how
does a multitude of orphans weep together
when each one speaks an alien tongue?

Did you tell your name to the others, teach them
how to pronounce it? Or did you keep on forgetting
everything, including those you brought to life
and could not name?

JAMAICA

above all
taste

of ac-
cent
taste

of red village in
bauxite dirt
taste

of soap sud drying
on limestone rock

above all
taste

of things sun
boils away

NOTES ON THE TEXT

* In Jamaica, the large, flat, gently sloping stone structure on which coffee is dried is called a barbecue. I spent my childhood living between a district called Coffee Grove and a small town called Porus in central Jamaica.

* 'Brother' and 'Sister' are forms of address for members of churches and other faith groups in Jamaica. These are particularly essential when the person being addressed is an elder.

* Mama is the name of the grandmother.

* In 'smile of leeches perfect circle', the italicised lines have been borrowed from Leon Gontran Damas's *Black Label*.

* The K-Fêt is the actual name of the student café at the École normale supérieure on rue d'Ulm in Paris. K-Fêt is a phonetic play on the word *cafette*, urban dimunitive of *cafétéria*.

* MCR – acronym for Middle Common Room, a term for both the graduate student body and the meeting room that is for their sole use in the colleges at the University of Oxford.

* The phrase '*Texte, mon corps*' is taken from Hélène Cixous' *Le rire de la Méduse*. The first lines in Italian in the opening sequence are from Luigi Pirandello's *Malgiocondo*. 'Self-Portrait as Othello V' paraphrases a line from Jack Halberstam's *In a Queer Time and Place*. In Part I, a few phrases in French have been taken from Aimé Césaire's essay 'Poésie et connaissance'.

* The extract from the voyage of Alvise Da Cada Mosto is taken from *Original Journals of the Voyages of Cada Mosto, and*

Pedro de Cintra, to the Coast of Africa, in Robert Kerr, *A General History and Collection of Voyages and Travels, Vol. II.* Edinburgh: William Blackwood; London: T. Cadwell, 1824.

* A number of other works have been instrumental in the composition of this book. Among them are Dionne Brand's *Map to the Door of No Return: Notes to Belonging* and Michael Brennan's work in progress entitled *English Travellers to Venice: 1450–1700,* encompassing c.30 travel accounts and their relationships to Anglo-Venetian cultural and political relations during this period.

ACKNOWLEDGEMENTS

Malika Booker, MIMI KHALVATI, Khadijah Ibrahiim, Jacob Ross, KWAME DAWES, CHARLES HENRY ROWELL, John McAuliffe, Roger Robinson, Naush Sabah, Nick Makoha, Gboyega Odubanjo, John Whale, Mick Gidley, Lucile Allen-Paisant, Jeremy Poynting, Zaffar Kunial, Andre Bagoo, Denise Saul, Colin Grant, Gregory Pardlo, Forrest Gander, Valerie Cassel Oliver, Howell Perkins and the Virginia Museum of Fine Art, Harriet Moore; Lisa Luxx (for the comment you made to me at Outspoken at the Southbank Centre); Isla Paterson and Evie Lewis (for inviting me to deliver a keynote at your 'Borders and Borderlands' conference).

Poems from this book have previously appeared in *Callaloo*, *The Poetry Magazine*, *Poetry Birmingham Literary Magazine*, *Magma*, and *Moko Magazine*.